Introduction
by Carole Cooper

So what else do I have to do but to write this fabulously simple cookbook which compiles the best of my recipes created over the many years of cooking for and feeding people who visited us at our Natural Food Store in Southern California -called Seacoast! My husband Geoffrey and I have been in the natural foods business for the past 30 years; selling vitamins, selling food and yes selling natural home cooked food in our Deli. After 30 years the vitamins have gone to cyberspace offering the world the best of the best in nutritional supplements via the internet. Our "Deli" is now my own kitchen overlooking the beautiful shores of Lake Superior at our Seacoast Lakeshore Resort in the Upper Peninsula of Michigan; our visitors are now family and friends who have encouraged me over these many years to write the recipes down!!

I hope you try the recipes, eat this healthy food and share the simplicity and joy of cooking with your family and friends! And remember always, Enjoy!

Simply Natural Gourmet

Dedicated to my husband Geoffrey and my little sister Joanna whose steadfast confidence in my abilities have always made me shine!
And a special thank you to my sister in law Sally whose gourmet cooking has always inspired me. And to all those customers and guests, friends and family that have tasted my creations and have told me to write them down.
I love you all!

Copyright 2012 by the author of this book,, Carole Cooper. The book author retains sole copyright to his or her contributions to this book.
ISBN # 978-0-9883944-0-7

Salads and Sides — Page

- Artichoke Feta Salad — 8
- Cuban Black Bean Salad — 9
- Curried Couscous Salad — 11
- Oriental Coleslaw — 12
- Pasta Artichoke Salad — 14
- Szechuan Salad — 16
- Santa Fé Three Bean Salad — 17
- Rice & Bean Salad — 19
- Dijon Potato Salad — 20
- Farro, White Bean and Artichoke — 23
- Tofu Salad — 25
- Cucumber Asparagus Salad — 27
- Cilantro Corn Salad — 29
- Balsamic Beets — 30
- Taboulie — 32
- Cucumber Tomato salad with roasted squash — 35

Pasta

- Pasta w/Roasted Pumpkin and Black Beans — 37
- Linguine with Clam Sauce — 38
- Spaghetti with Beets — 39
- Chicken Cappellini with Artichokes — 40
- Pasta with Greens — 43
- Spinach Fettuccine with Bacon, Parsnips & Peas — 45
- Linguine with Tuna, Spinach & Lemon — 47
- Spaghetti w/Fried Zucchini and Anchovy Sauce — 49
- Bucatini w/Sardines and Fennel — 50

Entrées	Page
Eggplant Zucchini Casserole	53
Potato Artichoke Casserole	54
Vegetarian Dolma	55
Chicken Rosemary	58
Vegetarian Enchilada	60
Spanish Paella	62
Tofu and Vegetable Stir Fry	64
Grilled or Baked WhiteFish	66
Olive Oil Poached Tuna	68
with salsa verde	69
and Potato/Tomato Medley	70
The Holiday Turkey	71
Moroccan Grilled Flank Steak	74
Roast Leg of Lamb	75
Oven Baked Pork Roast w/fennel	77
and shitake mushroom	
Moroccan Chicken Tagine	79
Italian Summer Stew	80

Simply Natural Gourmet

Salads & Sides

Simply Natural Gourmet

ARTICHOKE FETA SALAD

I found this dish in a greek restaurant in Detroit in the early 70's-Have been hooked ever since!

4 cups of artichoke hearts(quartered)
8 firm but ripe roma tomatoes(quartered)
2 cans garbanzo beans(rinsed and drained)
1 cup greek olives(colossal or kalamata)
16 oz brick feta cheese(cubed)
1 cup extra virgin olive oil
4 tsp dried oregano leaves
2 tsp granulated garlic
1 tsp black pepper(medium grind)

Combine all ingredients, except oil, in a shallow heat proof pan
toss gently
heat oil in a saucepan just before smoking point(be careful not to burn it)
carefully pour the hot oil over the ingredients(it will sizzle)
The flavors of the spices and herbs will lock into the vegetables and cheese after sizzling subsides.
serve with a basket of hot crusty bread and a bottle of dry red or white wine
This dish is a real party pleaser! The recipe will serve 10-12. You may cut ingredients in half to make a smaller portion.

Simply Natural Gourmet

CUBAN BLACK BEAN SALAD

3 cans black beans(rinsed and drained)
1 large red onion(chopped)
2 bunches fresh cilantro(minced)
3 medium carrots(diced)
1 red bell pepper(diced)
1 yellow bell pepper(diced)
1 pkg frozen corn kernels(thawed)
1 Tbls ground dried cumin
1/2 Tbls ground dried mustard
1 tsp granulated garlic
1/2 cup extra virgin olive oil
1/2 cup lemon or lime juice

Combine all ingredients in a large mixing bowl and mix thoroughly
slightly chill, if desired.

This dish may be served chilled or at room temperature. Delicious as a side to poultry, fish or pork tenderloin; serves 8-10.

This dish may be served chilled or at room temperature. Spice it up with a bit of tabasco or salsa, for those who like it hot!

As a stand alone meal, can be rolled in corn or flour tortillas and served burrito style; serves 6-8.

Makes a great salad all alone.
This is a very delicious and versatile dish!

Simply Natural Gourmet

CURRIED COUSCOUS SALAD

1 1/2 cups couscous or 1 pkg of couscous(Fantastic Foods, Casbah or Near East)
3 cups water
1 red bell pepper(chopped)
2 fresh cilantro(minced)
1 1/2 pkg of frozen mixed vegetables(cascadian gardener's blend or other)
2 TBLS curry powder
1 tsp granulated garlic
1/2 cup extra virgin olive oil

Bring water to boil, add couscous, stir, remove from heat and let stand(covered) for 5 minutes
In a large mixing bowl, combine couscous with all other ingredients
gently toss
add more curry powder to taste and olive oil to moisten,if needed

This salad has a delightful mild curry flavor.
As a side dish, it makes a perfect compliment to poultry or pork,serves 8-10.
Alone, it is a flavorful light entrée; perfect on a hot summer day
As an entrée, serves 4-6
Enjoy!

Simply Natural Gourmet

ORIENTAL COLESLAW

A nutritious and delicious macrobiotic dish

1 napa cabbage(finely chopped)
3 carrots(shredded)
1 cup mung bean sprouts
1 bunch parsley or cilantro(minced)
3-4 sheets of nori seaweed(torn into shreds)
1/4 cup toasted sesame oil
1/2 cup tamari or soy sauce
juice of 1 whole lemon
dash of cayenne pepper
1 tsp kelp powder

In a large mixing bowl, combine all ingredients
toss gently

Simply Natural Gourmet

Serve the coleslaw on a platter or in a shallow bowl.
As a side dish, makes a great companion to chicken or pork; serves 8-10.
To make this salad an entrée, see variations.

Variations for entrée versions:
May substitute the nori for 1 cup refreshed hijiki seaweed(refresh by soaking hijiki in water for 20 minutes, then drain)
Hijiki will give this salad more substance for a vegetarian entrée.

Add strips of cooked chicken or turkey breast to the nori or hijiki versions.

Add boiled and peeled medium shrimp or shredded crab to the nori version.
Any way you serve it, it's sure to be a surprising hit.
Enjoy!

Simply Natural Gourmet

PASTA ARTICHOKE SALAD

1 lb. pasta(rotini,farfale,ziti,penne or rigatoni)
1 16 oz can waterpacked artichoke hearts,drained and quartered
1 16 oz can pitted black olives
1 red bell pepper,chopped
1 bunch fresh basil,chopped
2 zucchini,chopped
1 med. red onion, chopped
1 8 oz pkg. feta cheese, crumbled
2 Tbls balsamic vinegar
1/4 cup red wine vinegar
1/4 cup extra virgin olive oil
1 tsp dried oregano leaves

Simply Natural Gourmet

1/4 tsp black pepper
pinch of granulated garlic (optional

Bring a large pot of water to a boil (salt optional)
Place pasta in water and cook until "al dente"(firm)
Drain in colander
In a large mixing bowl combine pasta and all other ingredients
Toss gently and chill slightly

The feta cheese and artichoke combination give this salad true Mediterranean flavor.
Arrange the finished pasta salad on a platter or shallow bowl.
Can be served alone,as a light entrée; or as a side dish is a perfect complement to grilled lamb, fish or chicken.
Enjoy Serves 4-8

SZECHUAN SALAD

Soft noodles and crispy vegetables, infused with oriental spices.

2 pkgs udon noodles(EDEN or other brand)
1 small can of baby corn(rinsed and drained; cut corns in half)
1 can sliced water chestnuts(rinsed and drained)
1/2 cup fresh china pea pods(remove strings)
1 red bell pepper(chopped)
2 green onions(chopped)
1 cup bok choy(chopped in large pieces)
1 cup napa cabbage(chopped), optional
1/2 cup szechuan sauce(we prefer SAN-J)
2 Tbsl toasted sesame oil
1/4 cup tamari sauce(preferably lo-sodium)

Bring large pot of water to a boil; add noodles, cook until firm and drain.
In a large mixing bowl, combine cooked noodles with the vegetables, corn and chestnuts.
Add szechuan sauce, oil and tamari
toss gently
serve warm, chilled or room temperature.

This is a very delicious but spicy oriental dish.
A great vegetarian entrée but a perfect complement to grilled fish or chicken as well.
Makes a delightful cold summer salad.
serves 6-8 easily

Simply Natural Gourmet

SANTA FÉ THREE BEAN SALAD

16 oz can garbanzo beans
16 oz can kidney beans
1 kg frozen green beans
1 yellow bell pepper, chopped
1 red bell pepper, chopped
1 bunch fresh cilantro, chopped
1 medium red onion, chopped
tsp ground cumin
tsp ground turmeric
tsp granulated garlic
1/2 tsp sea salt
1/2 tsp medium cracked black pepper
2 Tbls organic cane sugar

Simply Natural Gourmet

1/2 cup cider vinegar
1/4 cup extra virgin olive oil

Drain and Rinse canned beans
In a large mixing bowl combine beans with rest of ingredients, toss with seasonings, vinegar and olive oil. adjust seasonings to taste

Serve room temperature or slightly chilled in a bowl or platter. As individual salads, pile on top of romaine lettuce leaves arranged on individual salad plates. Enjoy with a grilled entrée. Serves 4-6
15 minute preparation time!

Simply Natural Gourmet

RICE AND BEAN SALAD

This is a particularly healthy dish. The combination of rice and legumes make a perfect vegetarian protein.

3 cups cooked brown rice
1 can each of garbanzo, kidney and cannellini beans (rinsed and drained)
1 large red bell pepper (diced)
2 green onions(diced)
3 medium carrots(diced)
1 cup diced celery
2 yellow crookneck squash(diced)
2 Tbls Modern Spike Seasoning
1 Tbls dried dill leaves
1 cup Caesar Cardini's lemon dressing (or similar)

Combine all ingredients in a large mixing bowl
stir in dressing and chill

Simply Natural Gourmet

This delightfully healthy dish stands alone as an entrée providing protein, carbohydrates and fats.
It is a great potluck party pleaser; serves 10-12 or more
If used as a side dish, better served with a light grilled fish or poultry rather than a red meat.

Simply Natural Gourmet

Dijon Potato Salad

8 red, yellow finn or yukon gold potatoes
1 medium red onion , chopped
1 green bell pepper , chopped
1 red bell pepper, chopped
1 & 1/2 cup chopped celery
2 medium carrots, chopped
1/2 cup prepared dijon mustard
1 TBLS dried dill leaves
1 tsp spike seasoning
1/2 tsp medium grind black pepper
1/2 cup extra virgin olive oil

Boil potatoes, let cool and cube

Simply Natural Gourmet

In a large mixing bowl combine potatoes with rest of chopped vegetables; add mustard, seasonings and olive oil Mix thoroughly and chill for 1 hour

Shed the mayonnaise with this delightful, low calorie alternative potato salad. Serve as you would any potato salad, you won't miss the mayo!! Easily serves 4-6 Enjoy!

Simply Natural Gourmet

FARRO, WHITE BEAN AND ARTICHOKE SALAD

1 & 1/2 cup semi-pearled Farro
1/4 cup extra virgin olive oil
1 lemon, juiced and outer peel finely shredded
1 medium sweet onion
1/2 cup matchstick carrots
1 cup chopped celery
1 cup low sodium chicken broth
1 can cannellini beans, drained and rinsed
1 can artichoke hearts, drained and quartered
1 cup grape tomatoes, halved
1 cup flat leaf parsley, chopped
1 tsp dried peppermint leaves
1 tsp greek seasoning

Simply Natural Gourmet

freshly ground salt and pepper to taste

Boil Farro until just tender, about 10 minutes
Drain and add farro to skillet with half of the olive oil, onions, celery and carrots and lemon zest
sauté about 5 minutes
add the chicken broth, white beans, artichokes and seasonings
simmer another 3 minutes
add parsley, tomatoes, lemon juice and remaining olive oil
salt and pepper to taste.
Transfer to serving bowl with lid

Serve this dish as a room temperature side dish or cold salad. Particularly delicious with Leg of Lamb! Also sensational as a stand alone vegetable entrée.

You may substitute the chicken broth for vegetable broth to make a vegan version!

Farro (an ancient Italian wheat) is a very versatile, delicious and nutritious grain full of fiber and minerals.

A good for you grain! Serves 4-6. Enjoy!

Simply Natural Gourmet

Tofu Salad a la Seacoast

2 lbs of extra firm tofu, cubed
3 large organic carrots, sliced
1/2 head of celery, chopped medium
3 green onions, chopped
2-3 summer squash(yellow crookneck or zucchini), chopped medium
1 sweet red pepper, chopped medium
1/2 cup tamari sauce
1/2 cup extra virgin olive oil
3/4 cup nutritional yeast
1/2 cup raw sunflower seeds
1 tsp ground cumin
1 tsp dried dill
1 tsp spike seasoning
1 tsp granulated garlic
parsley or cilantro for garnish

Simply Natural Gourmet

In a large bowl mix all the ingredients together and transfer to a shallow serving dish, garnish with coarsely chopped flat leaf parsley or cilantro. Serves 4-6.

I cannot even try to guess how many pounds of this delicious, nutritious salad our Deli sold over the years! It simply was the best seller. It really is a stand alone vegan meal full of protein, vitamins and minerals and it tastes great!! Enjoy!

Simply Natural Gourmet

Cucumber Asparagus Salad

Crisp cucumber slices and raw asparagus usher in Spring's lighter fare; perfectly accompanies spring lamb or chicken breasts- yummy all on it's own.

2-3 crisp cucumbers, diagonally sliced
1 bunch medium asparagus, diagonally sliced
1 red bell pepper, thinly sliced
1/4 cup extra virgin olive oil
1 lemon, (zest the peel and juice the fruit)
1/2 tsp dried dill(mint may be used as an alternative)
1/2 tsp dried oregano
flat leaf parsley, coarsely chopped

Simply Natural Gourmet

In a large bowl,combine all the ingredients, toss and transfer to a shallow serving dish. Serve with the above mentioned choice of meat or thinly sliced grilled flank steak; also perfect as a starter salad! Serves 4-6. Enjoy!

Simply Natural Gourmet

Cilantro Corn Salad

This summer fresh salad is an excellent side to an array of grilled meats and poultry!

2 lb bags of frozen corn kernels
2 bunches of fresh cilantro, chopped
1 large red onion, chopped
1 orange bell pepper, chopped
1/4 cup extra virgin olive oil
juice of one lemon
1/4 tsp ground cumin
pinch of red pepper flakes(or chipotle pepper flakes)
freshly ground salt and pepper to taste

In a large bowl mix together all ingredients. Transfer to a shallow serving dish.

Serve with grilled pork , grilled steak or grilled chicken breasts.

Also may be served as a side to corns game hens, turkey or whole roasted chicken.

Will serve 6-8 depending upon how you serve it!
Enjoy!

Simply Natural Gourmet

Balsamic Beets

A simple, nutritious side dish or salad in any season. Wonderful as an accompaniment to roasted turkey or chicken.

6-8 medium/large beets, peeled and sliced
granulated garlic to taste
dried oregano to taste
freshly ground salt and pepper to taste

Simply Natural Gourmet

a drizzle of extra virgin olive oil
a splash of balsamic vinegar

Steam beets in a medium sized saucepan until fork tender
drain cooked beets
In a medium bowl toss cooked beets with remaining ingredients.
Transfer to serving dish. Serves 4-6

This dish may be served warm or at room temperature.
Enjoy!

Simply Natural Gourmet

Taboulie

A middle eastern favorite that became a staple salad for natural food lovers. Stands alone beautifully but also compliments a variety of meat entrées and especially lamb dishes.

1 cup boiling water
2 cups bulgur wheat
2 cups flat leaf parsley, finely chopped
4 firm tomatoes, seeded and finely chopped
1 large sweet onion, minced
juice of 2 lemons
3/4 cup extra virgin olive oil
3-4 Tables of fresh mint or 2 Tables dried mint

Simply Natural Gourmet

freshly ground salt and pepper to taste.

In a large bowl pour boiling water over bulgur and let set for at least 1 hour. Add remaining ingredients to the bulgur, mix thoroughly and refrigerate for at least 1 hour.

Taboulie holds up well refrigerated for several days. Serves 6-8. Delicious and nutritious. Enjoy!

Simply Natural Gourmet

Cucumber,Tomato Salad with Roasted Squash

Simply Natural Gourmet

1 medium delicata squash, sliced
4-5 green tomatoes, quartered
5-6 large radish, sliced
Grind to salt(frontier herb blend)
dash of roasted coriander
ground pepper
olive oil

2 seedless or slicing cucumbers, sliced
3-4 firm heirloom tomatoes, quartered
fresh ground salt and pepper
juice of one lime and zest

In a sheet pan arrange squash, green tomato and radish
season with "grind to salt", coriander and pepper
dredge with olive oil
roast at 425 degrees for 25 minutes until squash is crisp tender, occasionally tossing

In a serving platter, arrange the cucumber and heirloom tomato
top with the roasted vegetables
sprinkle with the lime zest and lime juice
salt and pepper to taste

This is a very satisfying salad and can stand alone or be served with a grilled meat. Perfect in the late summer when the vegetables are at their peak. Enjoy!

Simply Natural Gourmet

Pasta

Simply Natural Gourmet

Pasta w/Roasted Pumpkin and Beans

This is a no rules pasta dish! you can use any kind of macaroni cut you prefer, pumpkin can be substituted for any variety of squash (winter or summer) and the beans can be either black or white; cilantro or flat leaf parsley, thyme or sage, garlic or shallots . In this version I will use roasted pumpkin and black beans with a cilantro garnish!

1 medium cooking pumpkin (peeled and cubed)
1 kg grape tomatoes
6 cloves garlic(whole)
fresh ground salt and pepper
dash of red pepper flakes
dash of Old Bay seasoning
1/4 tsp dried thyme leaves
a drizzle of extra virgin oil
I pkg of macaroni (I like casarecce)
1 can of black beans(rinsed)
one bunch fresh cilantro(chopped)
parmesan or feta cheese for garnish

Combine 1st 8 ingredients in a shallow baking dish roast for 25 minutes at 425 farenheit until pumpkin is fork tender, meanwhile boil pasta in salted water until al dente; drain and reserve at least 1 cup of the cooking liquid just in case you need it; add pasta to the roasted vegetables and toss with the black beans and chopped cilantro, add a bit of cooking liquid if too dry
serve with shaved parmesan or crumbled feta cheese
this dish is delicious!! Enjoy

Simply Natural Gourmet

Simple Linguine with Clam Sauce

Simply Natural Gourmet

I have been making this clam sauce for many years. It is so simple to prepare but full of flavor and a real crowd pleaser!

Extra virgin olive oil(enough to coat the pan)
2-3 cloves garlic, chopped
1 28 oz can of whole tomatoes (cut up tomatoes or use a can of prediced)
2 cans of whole baby clams (drained but reserve the clam liquid)
2 tsp medium ground black pepper(yes its a lot)
pinch of salt
1 bunch flat leaf parsley, chopped
12 -16 oz linguine

In a large skillet, saute garlic in the olive oil until soft and fragrant on medium high heat
add the reserved clam juice
add the tomatoes, black pepper, salt
simmer for about 15 minutes, then add clams and parsley
simmer an additional 15 minutes

In the meantime cook linguine in boiling salted water until al dente
drain the pasta and serve with the clam sauce

Top with shaved parmesan or seasoned breadcrumbs (see recipe)
Enjoy!

Spaghetti with Beets

This is a vegetarian pasta dish that is absolutely delicious, nutritious and fun to make!

6 medium/large sized beets
3-4 cloves garlic, minced
1/4 cup extra virgin olive oil (enough to coat the pan)
crushed red pepper flakes to taste
fresh ground salt to taste
1 lb of spaghetti, linguine or fettuccine

Heat oven to 425 degrees fahrenheit
wash and trim beets, wrap them in foil and place on a baking sheet; roast beets for about 45 minutes until fork tender; remove beets from foil and cool, peel and coarsely chop, set aside
in a very large skillet saute the garlic in the olive oil on medium high heat until soft and fragrant.
Add the red pepper, salt and beets and simmer for 8-10 minutes; remove the pan from heat

Meanwhile cook the pasta in boiling salted water until al dente; drain the pasta and reserve at least 1 cup of the cooking liquid. Stir the pasta into the beet mixture in the pan; and If too dry add the reserved cooking liquid. The pasta will take on the red color of the beets. Serve with shaved parmesan or seasoned breadcrumbs. Enjoy!
You may also sauté chopped beet greens (if fresh) into the mixture as a nutritious variation. Another variation, add roasted scarlet turnips along with beets. Delicious!

Simply Natural Gourmet

My Husband Geoffrey's Favorite Pasta Dish!

Chicken Cappellini with Artichokes and Capers

A very simple pasta dish that my family just raves about!
1 package of boneless, skinned chicken breasts
course ground salt and pepper to taste
1/4 cup flour
1/3 cup extra virgin olive oil
1&1/2 cup chicken broth
1 can artichoke quartered artichoke hearts(drained)
2 Tbls of capers (do not rinse)
dash of crushed red peppers flakes
1 bunch flat leaf parsley, chopped
i pkg Cappellini. angel hair pasta or thin Spaghetti

kosher salt
shaved parmesan

With a meat mallet, pound the chicken breasts until they become thin cutlets, set aside.
in a shallow dish mix flour with salt and pepper
add the chicken cutlets to the flour mixture, coat and shake off excess flour

Heat the olive oil in a large skillet at medium high heat
add the cutlets and brown on both sides, transfer cutlets to a dish and set aside.
In the same pan at medium high heat add the chicken broth, artichoke hearts and capers, and crushed red pepper,add back the chicken cutlets with any juices that have accumulated.
Simmer the mixture for at least 10 minutes
until chicken is cooked through, add the parsley

in the meantime bring a pot of salted water to a boil;
add the cappellini or spaghetti and cook until al dente;
drain and reserve at least one cup of the cooking liquid.

Toss a little olive oil with the pasta and divide into shallow pasta dishes.
Add the cooking liquid to the chicken mixture and stir.
Serve chicken cutlet and vegetable mixture on top of pasta , garnish with shaved parmesan if desired.

Just Delicious! Enjoy!

Simply Natural Gourmet

Pasta with Greens

You can't get simpler than this one! A nutritious vegetarian quick meal adaptable to many variations.

1 pkg pasta of your choice
kosher salt
3-4 bunches of greens (swiss chard, lacinto kale, dandelion greens, collards or a mixture of several kinds chopped
1/4 cup extra virgin olive oil
4 garlic cloves, minced
crushed red pepper to taste
fresh ground salt and black pepper
shaved parmesan or romano cheese

In a large skillet heat olive oil on medium high heat
add garlic and saute until soft, add crushed red pepper
add chopped greens and stir fry until tender
add salt and pepper

In the meantime add pasta to boiling salted water and cook until al dente; drain and reserve more than 1 cup of cooking liquid

Add the pasta to skillet; add the cooking liquid and stir to combine.
Serve immediately with shaved cheese.

There are so many variations to this recipe. To keep it vegetarian but to punch up the protein just add a drained can of cannellini beans.

Simply Natural Gourmet

Adding thinly sliced proscuitto to the greens while stir frying adds a lot of flavor and the addition of the cannellini beans makes it even more nutritious.

If you add oil cured black olives or Kalamata olives the taste is superb!!

Forget the proscuitto and instead add anchovy or sardines; the olives and anchovy work well together.

Just have fun with this recipe. It's great however you choose to make it. Serve with a simple Caesar Salad and Enjoy!

Simply Natural Gourmet

Spinach Fettuccine with Bacon, Parsnips and Peas

This is another yummy, light pasta dish that's a family favorite! I use naturally cured bacon from our local CSA Farm which keeps this dish healthy yet with all the flavor that a cured meat provides.

1 lb spinach fettuccine
1/2 lb naturally cured bacon, chopped
2 parsnips, peeled and sliced
1 small onion, chopped
1 package frozen peas
2-3 roma tomatoes, coarsely chopped
1-2 bunches of fresh arugala, chopped
fresh ground smoked black pepper
fresh ground salt
parmesan cheese for serving

In a large skillet (13 inch or more) sauté the bacon at medium high heat
then add the onion and parsnips and cook until vegetables are crisp tender
add the peas and tomatoes and cook a few minutes longer on low heat

Meanwhile, bring a large pot of salted water to a boil and cook fettuccine until al dente, drain and reserve 1 cup+ of the cooking liquid
Add the fettuccine to the skillet, add the arugala, mix thoroughly, salt and pepper to taste

Simply Natural Gourmet

Add enough reserved cooking liquid to form a thin sauce
Serve immediately with shaved parmesan cheese.

This is really a delightfully delicious and light dish. Enjoy!

Simply Natural Gourmet

Linguine with Tuna, Spinach & Lemon

An absolutely delicious Pasta Dish!

1 lb Linguine
1/2 cup olive oil
zest of 2 lemons, juice of 2 lemons
1 head of garlic, peeled and minced
1/2 tsp crushed red pepper
2 cans water packed albacore tuna, drained
2 cans olive oil packed tuna, undrained
4-6 cups baby spinach
fresh ground salt & pepper to taste

Cook linguine in a large pot of salted water until al dente
Meanwhile heat the olive oil in a very large skillet on medium high
Add minced garlic and rushed red pepper and sauté for 2 minutes
Lower heat and add tuna, lemon juice and lemon zest
Drain linguine and reserve 1 cup cooking liquid
Add linguine and spinach to skillet, toss gently
Add reserved cooking liquid to desired consistency
Transfer to a shallow serving dish and serve immediately

Delicious with a tossed salad, crusty bread and a light white wine! Enjoy!

Spaghetti with Fried Zucchini and Anchovy Sauce

The egg yolks in this dish make a particularly luscious sauce!

3-4 small zucchini, sliced round
4 cloves garlic sliced
1/4 cup extra virgin olive oil
red pepper flakes to taste
lemon zest from half of large lemon (or one whole)
handful or torn basil
1/2 tin of flat anchovy, chopped including oil
2 egg yolks
1/2 cup of reserved salted pasta water
1/2 cup of finely shredded pecorino romano cheese
fresh ground black pepper
12 oz of spaghetti
1 cup reserved salted pasta water
1/2 cup chopped fresh chives
1/2 cup chopped fresh flat leaf parsley

Heat olive oil on medium high in a large fry pan
add zucchini and garlic and brown
add red pepper, lemon zest, torn basil leaves
add chopped anchovies and the oil from anchovy tin
lower heat

Meanwhile cook spaghetti in a large pot of boiling salted water
Reserve 1/2 cup water from pot while spaghetti is still cooking

Simply Natural Gourmet

In a small bowl whisk egg yolks in the reserved water add to zucchini mixture along with cheese and black pepper

When spaghetti is slightly undercooked, drain and reserve another cup of pasta water

Add spaghetti to the pan and mix to coat with the sauce add chives and parsley and pasta water
remove from heat and serve immediately with extra cheese if desired. This one is a keeper!!

Bucatini with Sardines & Fennel

This is my version of a traditional Sicilian pasta dish eaten on special occasions such as Christmas and Easter!!

1 lb Bucatini pasta
1/2 cup olive oil
2 large onions, sliced
1 large fennel, sliced thinly (bulb and fronds)
6 cloves garlic, roughly chopped
3 Tables tomato paste
1 28 oz can whole tomatoes, crushed with juices
large pinch of dried oregano
handful of chopped fresh basil
salt and pepper, fresh ground
4-5 anchovies, drained and chopped
4 cans of portuguese or french sardines, drained
1 cup golden raisins, soaked for 30 minutes, then drained
1/3 cup of pine nuts
1 tsp saffron soaked in warm water
1 bunch of flat leaf parsley, chopped
seasoned italian bread crumbs, prepared with olive oil

Simply Natural Gourmet

In a large skillet, heat the oil on medium high
add onions and garlic, brown
add fennel and cook for 3 minutes
add tomato paste and stir
add crushed whole tomatoes and all juices
add oregano and basil and anchovy
simmer for 30 minutes, stir occasionally

In the meantime bring a large pot of salted water to a
boil and cook Bucatini until al dente

Return to the sauce and add sardines, raisins, pine nuts
and the saffron with water

Drain Bucatini and add it to the sauce
stir to blend sauce with pasta
season to taste with ground salt and pepper and a pinch
of red pepper flakes(if desired)

Serve immediately with parsley garnish and seasoned
bread crumb sprinkles. Serve this dish with a simple
romaine salad and a good bottle of chianti wine.

This dish is eaten traditionally with seasoned bread
crumbs instead of cheese. To prepare bread crumbs,
simply mix them with a dried italian seasoning blend and
a bit of olive oil, mix thoroughly to blend flavors. the
breadcrumbs can be stored in the refrigerator indefinitely.

A simply delicious pasta dish, Enjoy!!

Simply Natural Gourmet

Entrées

51

Simply Natural Gourmet

Eggplant Zucchini Casserole

A simply delicious vegetarian casserole freshly made and was sold in our deli daily!

2 Eggplant, unpeeled and sliced medium thickness
4 zucchini, unpeeled and sliced medium thickness
3-4 tomatoes, sliced
1 bunch fresh basil, roughly chopped
2 tsp dried oregano
freshly ground salt and pepper
olive oil for dredging
breadcrumbs for dredging
1 cup grated parmesan cheese

Preheat oven to 425 degrees farenheit
Coat a shallow baking dish with olive oil, then sprinkle a thin layer of breadcrumbs
Layer the eggplant, zucchini and tomato and season the layers with the basil, oregano, salt, pepper, breadcrumbs and cheese
Repeat the layers and dredge occasionally with olive oil ending with breadcrumbs and cheese

Cover the casserole with foil and bake for 25 minutes
Remove foil and brown for another 10 minutes.

Serve with a fresh green salad, glass of red wine. Enjoy!

The leftover casserole can be easily reheated and enjoyed the next day or frozen and reheated!

Simply Natural Gourmet

Potato Artichoke Casserole

Another absolutely delightful vegetarian entrée freshly made and sold in our deli daily!

8-10 yukon gold or other yellow fleshed potato, sliced
2 cans of quartered artichoke hearts, drained
2 medium sweet onions, sliced
3-4 tomatoes, sliced
2 tsp dried dill
2 tsp died oregano
freshly ground salt and pepper
1 cup muenster cheese, grated
olive oil for dredging
breadcrumbs for dredging

Preheat oven to 425 degrees farenheit

Coat a shallow baking dish with olive oil, then sprinkle a thin layer of breadcrumbs

Layer the potato, artichoke, onion and tomato and season the layers with the dill, oregano, salt pepper, breadcrumbs and cheese
Repeat the layers and dredge occasionally with olive oil ending with breadcrumbs and cheese
Cover the casserole with foil and bake for 25 minutes
Remove the foil and brown for another 10 minutes

Serve with a fresh green salad and a glass of wine!
The leftover casserole can be easily reheated and enjoyed the next day or frozen and reheated!

Simply Natural Gourmet

Vegetarian Dolma

I have made these stuffed grapevine leaves for over thirty years for our deli, for weddings and many occasions.
Although I have categorized this dish as a vegetarian entrée, vegetarian dolma make a wonderful side dish, traditionally served with lamb.

Simply Natural Gourmet

2 jars of brine packed grapevine leaves
1/3 cup extra virgin olive oil
2 jars of brine packed grapevine leaves
3 cloves garlic, minced
1 medium onion, diced
1 large eggplant, peeled and diced
3 medium zucchini, diced
1 1/2 tsp dried dill
1 1/2 tsp dried oregano
1/3 cup extra virgin olive oil
1 cup cooked short grain brown rice
1 large can of plum tomatoes with juice, chopped
2 Tbls dried basil
freshly ground salt and pepper

Drain, rinse and dry grapevine leaves, set aside

In a large fry pan, heat olive oil at medium high
add garlic and onion and sauté
add eggplant and zucchini, dill and oregano
cook until vegetables are soft
combine with cooked brown rice, let rest

Preheat oven to 350 degrees farenheit
Coat a large shallow baking dish with olive oil

Assemble grapevine leaves by placing 1 teaspoonful of the rice mixture in the middle of each leaf, tuck sides in and roll to close. If you find there are small leaves, lay two or three flat and make as one.

Simply Natural Gourmet

Place rolled, stuffed grapevine leaves tightly next to each other in prepared baking dish.
Cover the dolma with chopped tomatoes, basil and ground salt and pepper.

Bake the dish for 45 minutes to 1 hour

Serve the dolma hot or cold as a side dish , especially good with lamb but also wonderful with beef or pork.
This version of dolma makes a wonderful
vegetarian entrée, serve with a greek style salad!
Just delicious! Dolma are so very versatile so
freeze the leftover dolma and serve in a pinch!

Rosemary Chicken with Roasted Potatoes and Onions

I was raised on this simple, traditional Italian style chicken dish; served at practically every special occasion always at weddings. Births, deaths and everything else in between claim the dish as well, It just works!

2 Chickens,cut up or 2 pkgs of precut chicken
3 sweet onions peeled and quartered
8-10 potatoes, scrubbed & quartered
2 tsp dried whole rosemary
1 tsp dried basil
fresh ground salt& pepper to taste
1/4 cup extra virgin olive oil

Preheat oven to 425 degrees farenheit
In a very large shallow baking dish arrange the chicken pieces, potatoes and onions

Sprinkle with rosemary, basil, salt & pepper
Lightly pour the olive oil over the entire dish
Bake until chicken is cooked through and golden brown and potatoes can be pierced easily with a fork and are nicely browned, about 1 1/2 hours.

You may need to reduce the heat to 400-375 degrees if chicken is browning too quickly.

Arrange on a shallow serving dish and serve with a large salad a a good bottle of wine!
On special occasions this dish is also served with a lightly sauced penne. If you prefer to serve the chicken with a pasta dish, you can omit the potatoes from the baking process.

Double or triple the recipe for a perfect party choice. It's a real party pleaser.

This is just fabulous chicken, Everyone you serve it to will enjoy it !!

This is just fabulous chicken, Everyone you serve it to will enjoy it !!

Simply Natural Gourmet

Oh My God these are delicious and so simple to prepare!
Packed with beans and rice and vegetables and encased in corn tortillas for a perfect vegetable protein!

4 cups of diced carrots, celery and onions
1/4 cup olive oil
2 cans of drained pinto beans
3 cups brown rice, cooked
2 tsp ground roasted cumin
2 tsp dried oregano
tsp chili pepper flakes
2 tsp garlic powder
Tamari sauce to taste
1 large pkg of corn tortillas
2 cans of enchilada sauce
sliced cheddar cheese

Vegetarian Enchiladas

Heat olive oil
Sauté diced vegetables
In a large bowl, mix vegetables with beans and rice
season with spices and add tamari to taste

Coat the bottom of a large glass baking dish with olive oil
then a layer of corn tortillas, rice

Simply Natural Gourmet

mixture, enchilada sauce and cheese slices. Continue layering with tortillas, rice mixture, enchilada sauce and cheese. finish layering with sauce and cheese.

Bake in a preheated oven of **375** degrees farenheit until casserole is fork tender and bubbling, about **35** minutes.

Serve with a Caesar Salad and a good Spanish wine!

This one is a winner, Enjoy!!

Simply Natural Gourmet

Spanish Paella

Paella can be made in so many different ways and with a variety of meats as well as vegetables! Remember to always use either aborio rice or if you can find it a good Spanish rice such as Goya or Carnaroli and always use saffron!!

1 lb Chorizo or Italian sausage links(cut into chunks)
1 lb scallops
1 lb raw shrimp(deveined and peeled)
1 pkg chicken thighs or
2 cups precooked chicken(cut into chunks)
1/4 cup olive oil
1 head garlic(peeled and coarsely chopped)
1 large sweet onion(chopped)
1 large red bell pepper(chopped)
2 cups green beans or peas(or both)
2 cups aborio rice
4 cups of chicken broth
a good pinch of saffron threads
smoked sweet paprika to taste
freshly ground salt and pepper to taste
1 pkg of grape tomatoes

Simply Natural Gourmet

Start with a large paella pan or large fry pan
Heat oil in pan at medium high
add garlic onion and pepper
sauté until onions and garlic are brown
add sausage and chicken thighs (if using) and brown
add rice and stir until pearly white, about 2 minutes
add one cup of broth
add all the spices
lower to a medium simmer
stir occasionally until liquid is absorbed
add another cup of broth and allow liquid to absorb

At this point do not stir aggressively as you will want the the bottom of the pan to caramelize into a crust which is called the socarrat.

add the third cup of broth , scallops and shrimp
allow liquid to absorb
then add the last cup of broth, green beans and peas
add the chunks of precooked chicken(if using)
stir slightly
after the liquid is almost absorbed, scatter the grape tomatoes atop the paella
cover and remove from heat

let the paella rest for about 10 minutes

serve with a crisp cucumber salad and a good spanish wine.

You can't help but Enjoy this fabulous dish!!

Simply Natural Gourmet

Tofu and Vegetable Stir Fry

This one's a must if you've had a natural foods deli just remember to keep the vegetables super crisp and brown the tofu chunks so that the outer surface is crisp and the inside is soft.

1/4 cup of grape seed oil
dash of toasted sesame oil

Simply Natural Gourmet

1 Pkg of extra firm Tofu, cut in cubes and pat dried

3 cloves of garlic, roughly chopped
3-4 cups of assorted vegetables, good choices are carrots and daikon, sliced
one leek, sliced
bokchoy and red bell pepper, roughly chopped
broccoli florets
shitake mushrooms, roughly sliced
pinch of red pepper flakes
a dash of fish sauce
a good ready made stir fry sauce or tamari to taste

Start with heating oil in a stainless steal wok or chef pan with a flat bottom and high sides
get the oil really hot, add garlic
immediately add the tofu chunks, let brown and quickly but gently toss with a stir fry ladle
add all of the vegetables and continue to toss
add the fish sauce, pepper flakes and stir fry sauce or tamari

remove from heat and serve immediately atop a bed of rice or soba noodles

This stir fry pairs well with riesling or gewürztraminer wine or just a good cup of green tea!

Just Yummy!!

Simply Natural Gourmet

Our Resort is located on Lake Superior in The Upper Peninsula of Michigan where fresh Whitefish and Lake Trout are staples in the everyday diet! Needless to say we serve and eat a lot of very fresh fish!

Grilled or Baked Whitefish or Trout Fillets

Lake Superior Whitefish

2-4 fresh fish fillets
1 Tbls lemon grass herb
1 tsp herbs de provence
1 tsp fennel seed(whole)
1/2 tsp granulated garlic
fresh ground salt and pepper to taste
2 lemons, sliced thin
1 Tbls lemon juice
2 Tbls Bragg's liquid aminos

Place fish fillets on a baking sheet or grill pan
Season with the above ingredients.

If baking, preheat oven to 425 degrees farenheit and bake for 20 minutes

Lake Superior Trout

Simply Natural Gourmet

If you prefer to grill the fish fillets, use a hot grill and flip once (5 minutes on each side).
Turn the grill off, close lid of grill and let set for another 5 minutes.

Whether you choose the whitefish or the trout, Lake Superior fish is just so very sweet and delicious. The addition of fennel seeds augments the already natural sweetness of this locally caught fish!

Of course if you are unable to find either variety, you can use any firm, cold water fish.

These seasonings are wonderful on salmon fillets as well, just make sure the salmon is wild caught!

Serve the fish fillets with oven roasted potatoes and a fresh salad.

A basmati/wild rice pilaf is also a good side, with asparagus spears.

Penne primavera with broccoli, spinach and red pepper is another yummy sidedish to the fish.

A crisp white wine like sauvignon blanc is an excellent choice!

Serves 4-6

Enjoy!!

Simply Natural Gourmet

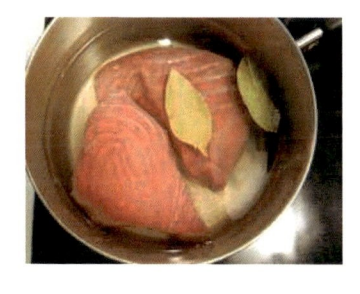

Olive oil Poached Tuna **Salsa Verde**

This is an absolutely fabulous tuna recipe! Though quick and easy to prepare, the results look as if you slaved over the stove all day! You may also use Halibut

Dress the tuna with a salsa verde and serve with a roasted potato, tomato and olive medley that is equally simple to prepare. Recipes follow...

4 Thick Tuna steaks
2 cups extra virgin olive oil
3 sprigs fresh rosemary or 1 tbls dried whole rosemary
4 cloves garlic, sliced
pinch of red pepper flakes

Heat olive oil in a large deep skillet to a low simmer
add rosemary and garlic slices
slip tuna steaks in the simmering oil and cook for 3 minutes on each side.

Remove tuna from oil, transfer to a flat plate or cutting board, let tuna rest for 10 minutes. You may reuse the

cooking oil; just decant in a glass jar and refrigerate. Slice tuna steaks against the grain and serve with salsa verde and roasted potato/tomato medley.
If using Halibut, serve the whole portion of fish without slicing.

Salsa Verde
one bunch fresh flat leaf parsley, coarsely chopped
one bunch fresh cilantro, coarsely chopped
one bunch fresh mint leaves, coarsely chopped
3-4 cloves garlic, chopped
1/4 cup of lemon juice
1/2 cup extra virgin olive oil

Combine all ingredients in a food processor and pulse just until blended. can be made ahead of time and stores in the refrigerator well.

Simply Natural Gourmet

Roasted Potatoes with Grape Tomatoes and Olives

This Mediterranean dish is delicious with olive oil poached tuna or halibut and is a lovely accompaniment to roasted or grilled lamb and is a perfect vegetarian entrée with a crisp salad and light wine!crisp salad and light wine!
2-3 lbs of new potatoes, halved or quartered
7-10 cloves of garlic, sliced in half
2 pints of grape or cherry tomatoes
1 cup olives, kalamata, oil cured, nicoise or spanish green
1/4 cup extra virgin olive oil
fresh ground salt and pepper to taste
pinch of red pepper flakes
lemon slices for garnish
preheat oven to 450 degrees farenheit

Place potatoes, tomatoes garlic and olives in a shallow baking dish or baking sheet, toss with olive oil and seasoning.

Bake for 25 minutes until potatoes are crisp tender and tomatoes are blistered. You may also grill this dish! Garnish with lemon slices and Enjoy!

The Salted Turkey

Everyone has their most perfect recipe for the holiday turkey and I have prepared this bird in a number of ways until I discovered the dry salt rub which in my opinion creates the most succulent meat encased in the brownest skin! Make sure you buy a farm raised turkey that has not been treated whatsoever!

1 16-19 lb Free Range Turkey
Herbed Salt consisting of:
1/3 cup kosher salt
1 tsp dried rosemary
1 tsp dried thyme
1 tsp dried sage
1 tsp dried oregano
2 tsp lemon zest
3 bay leaves
1 tsp whole peppercorns
1 large roasting bag

Simply Natural Gourmet

Salt the turkey as follows:
Mix the herbs, lemon zest and salt and pepper in a small bowl
Rinse the turkey thoroughly and do not pat dry
Place the turkey in the roasting bag
Sprinkle herb mixture on turkey and inside turkey cavity tie up bag and refrigerate for for 24 hours. You may want to place the bagged up turkey on a baking sheet.

Remove Turkey from bag and rinse turkey inside and out pat very dry.
Fill turkey cavity with 2 chopped lemons, 3 stalks of chopped celery and 2 sweet chopped onions.

Season turkey with the following choices:
2 Tbls oregano
2 Tbls thyme
1 tsp kosher or grey salt
1 tsp ground pepper
or
2 Tbls herbes de provence
1 Tbls sage
1 tsp kosher or grey salt
1 tsp ground pepper

Combine 1/2 cup extra virgin olive oil and 1/3 cup lemon juice in a small mixing bowl
brush turkey with half of the olive oil/lemon mixture reserve the rest for basting. the turkey can also be coated with butter
Place turkey in a large roasting pan with a rack;
tie legs together with kitchen string and tuck wing tips under. Pour 1 cup of wine and 1 cup of broth in bottom

Simply Natural Gourmet

of the pan. The broth can be premade from the neck and giblets of turkey; boil with onion, celery and carrot or use store bought low sodium chicken broth.

Roast turkey in bottom third of a preheated oven at 325-350 degrees farenheit
baste every 45 minutes until done, approximately 15-20 minutes per pound and 165-170 degrees farenheit on a meat thermometer.

Remove turkey from oven, transfer to a platter and let rest for 30-45 minutes.

Now make the gravy:
Place the roasting pan on two burners on stove top and bring to a slow boil at medium high add i cup of minced onion and 1/2 cup of flour or arrowroot and stir constantly until a roux is formed, then add 1 cup of white wine, 2 tbls of oregano or thyme and 1/2 cup of lemon juice. Keep stirring until the gravy is smooth and not too thick; salt and pepper to taste. Transfer gravy into a sauce pan and keep warm. Serve from a gravy boat.

The turkey is now ready to carve and serve with mashed potatoes, rice or sides of your choice with plenty of yummy gravy.

I use oregano and lemon juice in my gravy, however any herb of your choice will work. Try sage, thyme or rosemary or herbes de provence! Replace the the lemon with a dijon mustard and the herbs with garlic for another fabulous gravy! Explore your possibilities!

Simply Natural Gourmet

Feel free to use flat iron, hanger or skirt steak for this recipe! The cumin laden seasoning is a winner with all of these cuts of beef!

Moroccan Grilled Flank Steak

This steak delivers fabulous flavor and works well with many of the side dishes and salads in this book!
Taboulie or couscous salad would pair well with the meat as well as a large fresh green salad or simple sliced tomatoes and cucumbers! Don't forget the wine, a bold red is perfect!
Flank Steak, 2 -3 lbs
1 tbls roasted cumin
3 cloves garlic, minced
1 tbls moroccan seasoning (I like Victoria Gourmet)
1/2 tsp ras el hanout seasoning (Frontier)
1/4 cup extra virgin olive oil
Juice of 2 fresh limes
fresh ground salt and pepper to taste

Rub seasonings into steak with the olive oil and lime juice, let marinade for 1 hour at room temperature.
Grill to desired doneness, let meat rest for 20 minutes, slice against the grain.

Serve with a salad , above mentioned sides and wine.

Simply Natural Gourmet

A simply prepared leg of lamb takes no time at all but makes a magnificent presentation at table. A few simple herbs & lemon create an overwhelming flavor sensation!

Roast Leg of Lamb

Leg of lamb, 5-6 lbs1 bulb of garlic, cloves peeled and sliced1 bunch of fresh oregano, chopped
2 tbls of dried oregano
2 tbls kosher salt
fresh ground pepper to taste
Juice of 3 lemons
1/2 cup extra virgin olive oil

Preheat oven to 425 degrees farenheit
Coat the lamb with olive oil and lemon juice
With a sharp knife make small slits in the lamb and insert garlic slices throughout the lamb, rub remainder of the garlic all over the lamb along with the dried oregano salt and pepper,sprinkle fresh oregano all over the lamb
rest the lamb at room temperature for an hour

Place lamb in a roasting pan , add extra olive oil and lemon if needed.

Roast lamb for 45 minutes at 425 degrees, then reduce the oven temperature to 350 degrees and continue to

roast the lamb to desired doneness, 145 degrees on a meat thermometer for rare and 150-160 degrees for medium done!
Remove lamb from oven and let rest for 30 minutes

In the meantime oven roasted potatoes can easily be prepared in the same oven. Quarter potatoes, dress with olive oil, salt and pepper and a bit of dried dill. Roast in a shallow baking dish along side of the lamb or on the rack above!

The lamb can be served with potatoes and a fresh green salad!

A side of taboulie or couscous would be sensational!

Don't forget freshly sliced tomatoes and cucumbers with a bit of salt!

In the spring serve the lamb with orzo mixed with with roasted grape tomatoes and asparagus, laced with olive oil and lemon juice and salt and pepper!

This is a fabulous entrée that you will serve again and again. So easy and so simple and so enjoyable!

Try a Pinot Noir!

Simply Natural Gourmet

Bone in Pork Loin Roast with the addition of fennel and shitake mushroom make an extremely flavorful pork entrée that is lean and healthy. Serve with whole wheat couscous!!

Pork Roast w/Fennel and Shitake Mushroom

In the world of "health" pork, a very lean white meat, has gotten a bad rap. These days many local CSA farms humanely raise their own pigs that are fed a superb diet, so it is very easy to find pork products that are both lean and healthy! This recipe is sensational with the addition of fennel and shitake mushrooms that are roasted along side the pork, it is a winner!

Bone in pork loin, 5-6 lbs
2 medium fennel bulbs,sliced & fronds, chopped
3 cippolini onions, quartered
1 lb large shitake mushroom
2 tbls herbes de provence
extra pinch of dried whole rosemary
olive oil and balsamic vinegar
course ground salt and pepper
1/2 cup white wine

Preheat oven to 350 degrees farenheitPlace pork roast in a large roasting pan
Rub pork with herbs, salt and pepper and balsamic

Simply Natural Gourmet

vinegar,Dredge with olive oil and add the wine to pan.

Roast for 1 hour, covered with lid or aluminum foil and baste occasionally
Arrange onion, fennel bulbs and mushrooms around pork
You may also add carrots or parsnips to the mix if you wish.
Cover with aluminum foil or lid and roast the pork for at least 1 more hour, baste occasionally
A meat thermometer should read 170-180 degrees when pork is done.
Remove the vegetables from the roasting pan and set aside.
Uncover the roast; raise the oven to 450 degrees and brown the meat for 10 more minutes.

Transfer pork roast a carving board or platter and let rest for another 10 minutes.
Arrange vegetables around the meat. Serve with a whole wheat couscous and a crisp cabbage slaw
A good Chardonnay or Pinot Noir are perfect choices for this meal. Enjoy!

Simply Natural Gourmet

This traditional Moroccan dish is not only delicious but extremely healthful! Use a tagine cooking vessel, traditional Moroccan spices and serve with authentic basmati rice.

Moroccan Chicken Tagine

2-3 lbs free range chicken, cut up
2 Tbls Moroccan spice blend, Victoria's Gourmet
1 tsp Ras el Hanout spice blend, Frontier
2 large onions, sliced
3 carrots, sliced diagonally
1 or 2 preserved lemons, cut up
pinch of saffron threads
1/2 cup of low sodium broth
1/2 cup of pimento stuffed green olives
1/4 cup olive oil
fresh ground salt and grains of paradise pepper to taste

Heat olive oil in tagine on the stove top at medium high
Season the chicken with the spice blends and add to tagine
Brown the chicken as you turn it occasionally
Add onions and carrots and preserved lemon
Sprinkle with the saffron threads, add the broth and olives
Cover the tagine with lid and let simmer for 20-25

Simply Natural Gourmet

minutes.

Meanwhile make a pot of authentic basmati rice; I like Royal Brand as it is a very fine rice that elongates as it cooks. The rice should be fine and light and if you wish season it with a pinch of saffron and a bit of ground salt and a splash of olive oil for a superb flavor!
Serve the Chicken Tagine over the rice and enjoy a magnificent middle eastern dish that you will want to make again and again!
Enjoy with a good white wine such as unoaked chardonnay or a dry Riesling would be great as well!

A tagine is a Moroccan stew made in a cooking vessel by the same name. You can use beef or lamb in this recipe instead of chicken or you may use turkey tenders or parts as well.
The spices are very important; I find that the spice blends from Victoria's Gourmet or Frontier Co-op are perfect blends but you may use other blends or make your own just keep it authentic!

Simply Natural Gourmet

Italian Summer Vegetable Stew

I am finishing this cookbook with one of my husband's favorite recipes! He just loves this dish even though it is probably the simplest of all my recipes!

In the summer when home grown tomatoes and zucchini are abundant, I make a vegetable stew that my grandmother and mother made each year. they actually canned the stew so that we would have it year round! I make it fresh several times a month in the hot summer months and we just never get tired of eating it!

2-3 large zucchini, cut in chunks
6-7 potatoes, unpeeled and quartered
4-5 ripe tomatoes, chopped
1 large bunch of basil
1 large bunch of parsley
olive oil and a bit of water

Place all ingredients in a large stainless steal pan
Cook at medium high on stove top for about 10 minutes
Reduce to simmer for another 20 minutes

Serve it with pasta, rice or just eat it as is. it is a nutritious medley of the best of summer vegetables; add a side of Italian sausage or a can of French or Brisling sardines to complete the summer meal!

Oh and don't forget the wine!!
Enjoy, enjoy until we meet again!!

Simply Natural Gourmet

Italian Summer Stew with Zucchini, Potatoes and seasonal Tomatoes

Use seasonal summer vegetables and Heirloom Tomatoes

Simply Natural Gourmet

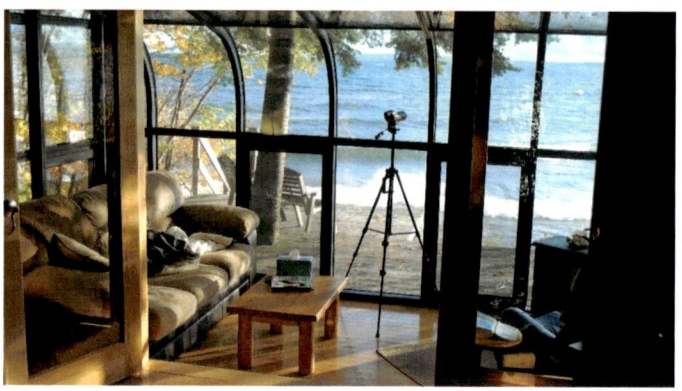

Seacoast Natural Foods and Seacoast Lakeshore Resort

Simply Natural Gourmet

Carole Cooper still cooking after all these years!

Seacoast Lakeshore Resort , Marquette Michigan 877 3076710